CAN YOU FIND A PLANET?

A Question of Science Book

CAN YOU FIND A PLANET?

by Sidney Rosen
illustrated by Dean Lindberg

 Carolrhoda Books, Inc. / Minneapolis

Each word that appears in **BOLD** in the text is explained in the glossary on page 40.

Text copyright © 1992 by Sidney Rosen
Illustrations copyright © 1992 by Carolrhoda Books, Inc.
Photographs reproduced courtesy of: cover, pp. 2-3, 12, 19, 21-24, 26-36, 37 (inset), 39, NASA/Jet Propulsion Laboratory; pp. 6-7, NOAO; p. 8, © Whit Bronaugh; p. 25, California Institute of Technology.

Carolrhoda Books, Inc., c/o The Lerner Group
241 First Avenue North, Minneapolis, Minnesota 55401

LIBRARY OF CONGRESS CATALOGING-IN-PUBLICATION DATA

Rosen, Sidney.
   Can you find a planet? / by Sidney Rosen ; with illustrations by Dean Lindberg.
       p.   cm. — (A Question of science book)
   Summary: Discusses in question and answer format the planets in our solar system and explains which planets and stars can be seen from Earth in the night sky.
   ISBN 0-87614-683-3 (lib. bdg.)
   1. Planets—Juvenile literature. [1. Planets. 2. Stars. 3. Questions and answers.] I. Lindberg, Dean, ill. II. Title. III. Series.
QB602.R66 1992
523.4—dc20   91-17943
                                                  CIP

Manufactured in the United States of America

2   3   4   5   6   7   –   P/MP   –   00   99   98   97   96   95

What's the trick to finding a planet?

The night sky is so full of pinpoints of light. It's not easy to tell a planet from a star. But let's begin with how to recognize a star.

Why begin with stars?

How many stars can we see in the sky at night?

That depends on where you are. City lights usually make it hard to see any but the very brightest stars. Out in the country, you can usually see many, many more. The ancient Greek **astronomer** Hipparchus made a list of about a thousand stars bright enough to see with the naked eye. How many stars can you count in the sky at night?

Because there are millions of stars in the sky. But there are only five planets you can see without a **telescope**. With a telescope, you can see three more planets.

So how can I tell planets from stars?

The first people to find the planets must have seen that a star always appears to be twinkling. A planet shines with a steady light. That's one difference.

What is another difference between stars and planets?

Planets move in the night sky. The ancient Greeks named them *planetes* (plah-ne-teys), which means "wanderers."

But don't stars move also?

Yes, but stars move in a special way. Imagine a bus where everyone has to sit in the same seat every day. Stars are like the people stuck on that bus. We see them move as a group without separating. A group of stars that moves like this is called a **constellation**.

But how can knowing about constellations help me find a planet?

What do constellations look like?

The star group that almost everyone knows is the one called *Ursa Major*, which means *Big Bear* in Latin. But to more modern eyes, the seven stars of this constellation look less like a bear and more like something you could use to dip water out of a bucket. We call it the Big Dipper.

A planet like Mars or Jupiter will slowly change its position, night after night. Little by little, it will move among the fixed stars of a constellation.

How else is a planet different from a star?

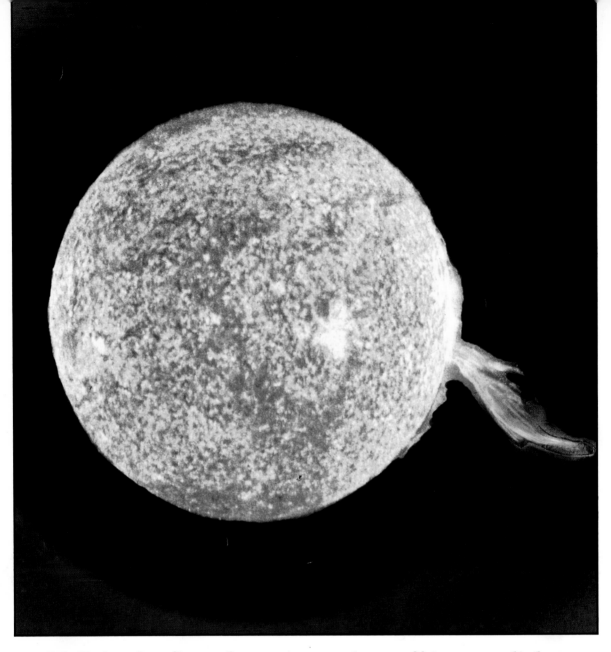

Well, in the first place, a star gives off its own light, just as our Sun does. All stars, including the Sun, are hot, burning balls of gas. Some may be larger or smaller, brighter or dimmer. But every star you see in the sky shines with its own light.

Don't planets shine, too?

Yes, but planets don't shine with their own light.
They are shining with the light of the Sun.
Sunlight bounces off the planet's surface just as light
is reflected by a mirror. The Sun's light is strong enough
for us to see even when it bounces back from Pluto,
the farthest planet in our **Solar System**.

Can we see light bouncing off any of the planets
in the daytime?

Yes. Mercury and Venus, the two planets nearest the Sun, are sometimes bright enough to be seen either just before sunset or just after sunrise.

Then, is a planet as bright as a star?

Planets are very bright compared to stars. And they may shine with different colors. Venus and Jupiter are a very bright yellow.

Mars has more of a reddish color.

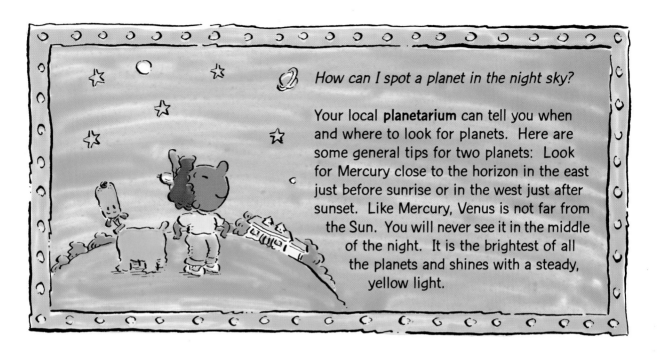

How can I spot a planet in the night sky?

Your local **planetarium** can tell you when and where to look for planets. Here are some general tips for two planets: Look for Mercury close to the horizon in the east just before sunrise or in the west just after sunset. Like Mercury, Venus is not far from the Sun. You will never see it in the middle of the night. It is the brightest of all the planets and shines with a steady, yellow light.

Saturn usually appears a little more purplish.

Star colors usually vary from a reddish yellow to a very bright blue-white.

Do other stars besides the Sun have planets?

Probably, but we don't know for sure. We can only
make a guess. If our star, the Sun, has planets going
around it, some of the other stars probably have
planets going around them, too.

How long would it take to get to another star?

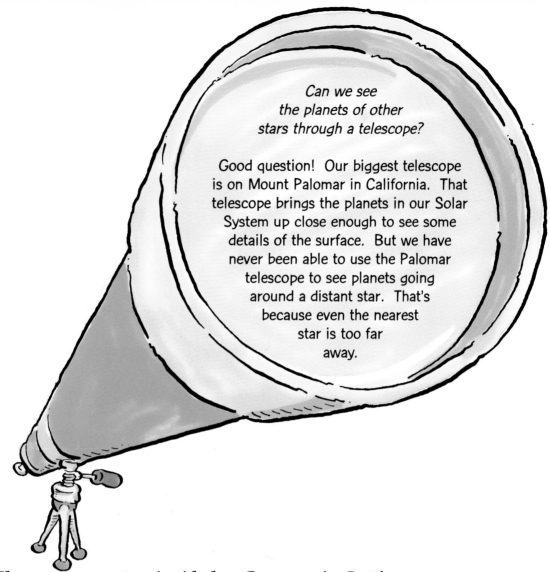

Can we see
the planets of other
stars through a telescope?

Good question! Our biggest telescope
is on Mount Palomar in California. That
telescope brings the planets in our Solar
System up close enough to see some
details of the surface. But we have
never been able to use the Palomar
telescope to see planets going
around a distant star. That's
because even the nearest
star is too far
away.

The nearest star is Alpha Centauri. Let's suppose you could take off in a rocket ship that could fly faster than any rocket ship has yet flown—with a speed of ten million miles an hour. When you arrived at Alpha Centauri, you would be more than two hundred and seventy years old, give or take a few years!

But what about the planets we can find in the sky? Can we visit them?

Oh, yes. But you'd have to hitch a ride on a rocket ship. And you might have to wait a while for a ride, because no one has ever gone to another planet.

How did we find out about the planets, if we haven't visited them?

Rocket ships without people in them have zoomed to all the other planets except Pluto. They sent back pictures of what the planets look like up close.

So, what have those rocket ships found?

Here's what they found on Mercury, the planet closest
to the Sun. Mercury is about as big as our moon.
Like the moon, it has neither air nor water. The side
of Mercury that faces the Sun is so *hot* that people
couldn't stay there. The other side is so *cold*,
they would freeze in a minute.

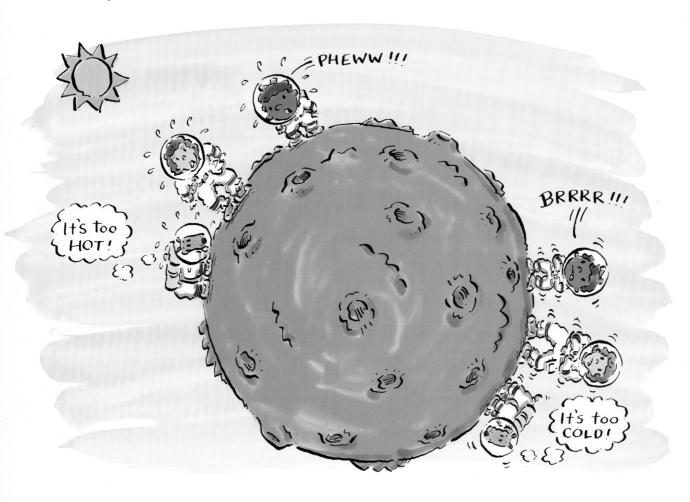

In 1974, the spacecraft *Mariner 10* managed to send
back about 4,000 pictures of Mercury's surface. To
no one's surprise, Mercury looked pretty much like the
moon, full of **craters** and high cliffs.

Venus is one of the most difficult planets to visit.

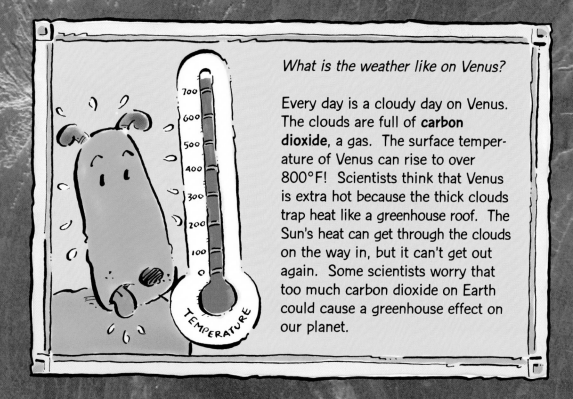

What is the weather like on Venus?

Every day is a cloudy day on Venus. The clouds are full of **carbon dioxide**, a gas. The surface temperature of Venus can rise to over 800°F! Scientists think that Venus is extra hot because the thick clouds trap heat like a greenhouse roof. The Sun's heat can get through the clouds on the way in, but it can't get out again. Some scientists worry that too much carbon dioxide on Earth could cause a greenhouse effect on our planet.

A heavy layer of clouds hides the surface. Early spaceships had trouble landing on Venus. The *Magellan* spacecraft, flying high above the planet, took this photo of the surface of Venus in 1990.

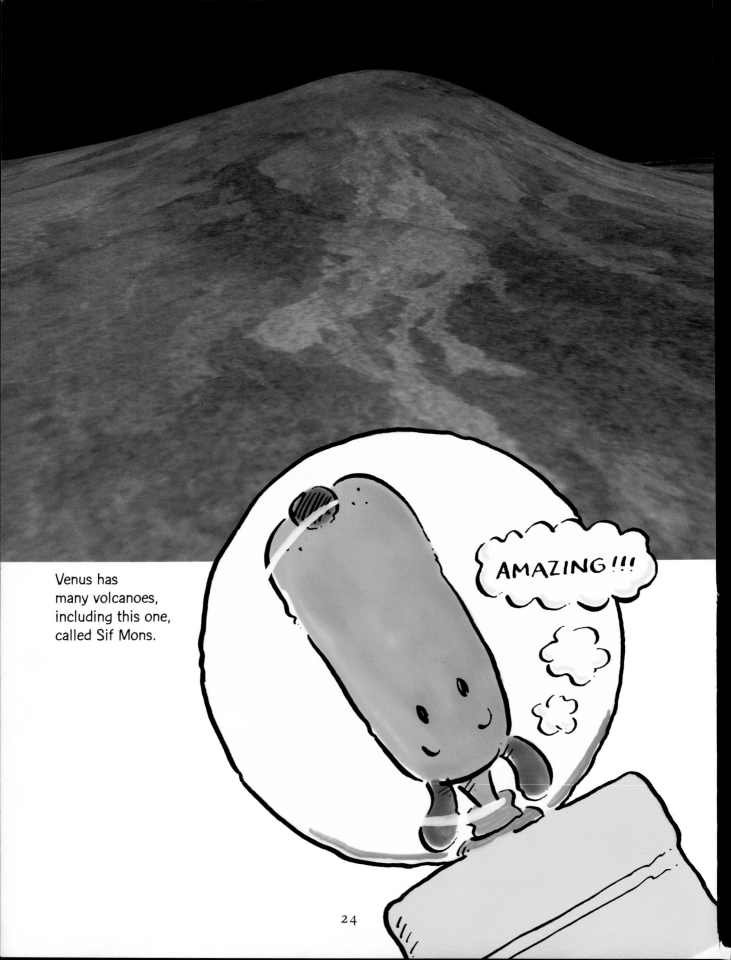

Venus has
many volcanoes,
including this one,
called Sif Mons.

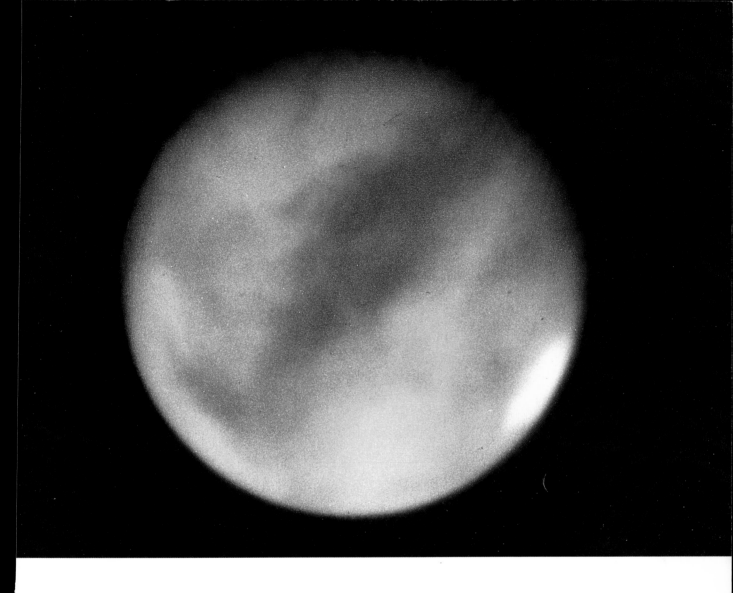

For a long time, Mars was a mystery to us. An American astronomer, Percival Lowell, looked through his telescope at Mars. He thought that lines on the planet's surface were great canals. Lowell decided that Martians built the canals to carry water around the planet. Pictures sent back by *Mariner 4* in 1964 told us that Lowell was wrong.

These pictures of Mars were sent back by *Viking 1,* which landed on the planet in 1976. A shovel on *Viking 1* dug up some Martian dirt for tests, but found no sign of life. The color of the Martian soil and rocks gives Mars its nickname, the Red Planet.

You can see a model of the Viking 1 lander on display at the National Air and Space Museum in Washington, D.C.

SEE THE
VIKING 1
DISPLAY

Largest of the planets, Jupiter appears to be a huge ball of swirling gas. If Jupiter were hollow, you could fit 1,000 planets the size of the Earth inside.

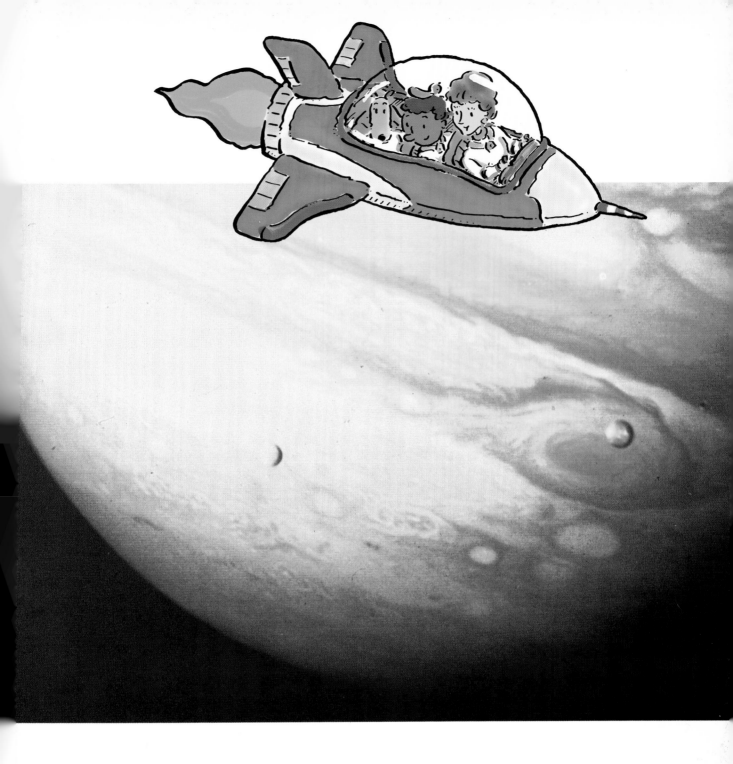

The best pictures of Jupiter were sent back by the
two *Voyager* spacecrafts, launched in 1977.

Voyager 1 sent back beautiful close-up photos of Jupiter's red spot. The Great Red Spot appears to be a great, ongoing hurricane made of gas.

Seen through a telescope, Saturn is one of the most beautiful sights in the sky. It looks like a purplish ball surrounded by several rings.

As the *Voyager* spaceships came closer, they showed us that there are more rings around Saturn than can be seen with a telescope. These rings seem to be made up of millions and millions of particles. Some of the particles are very, very tiny, and others are house-sized boulders.

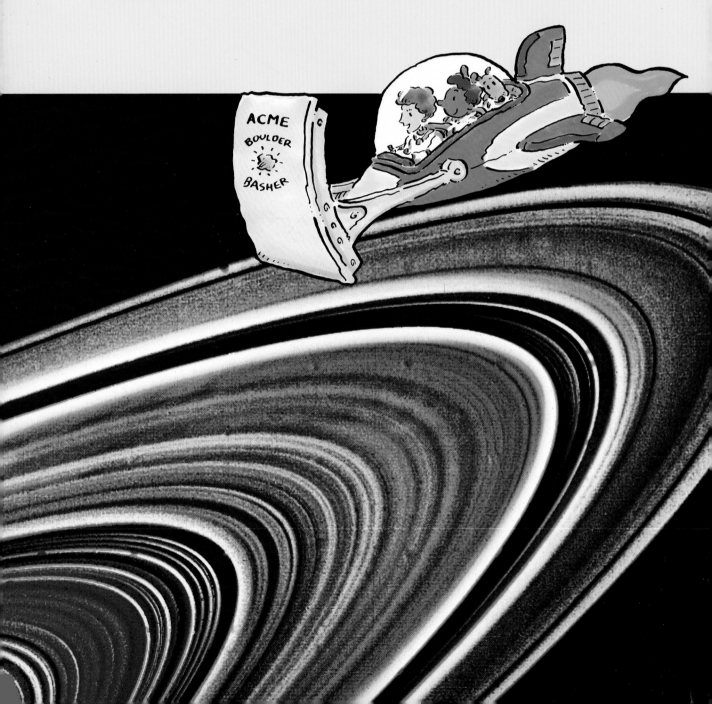

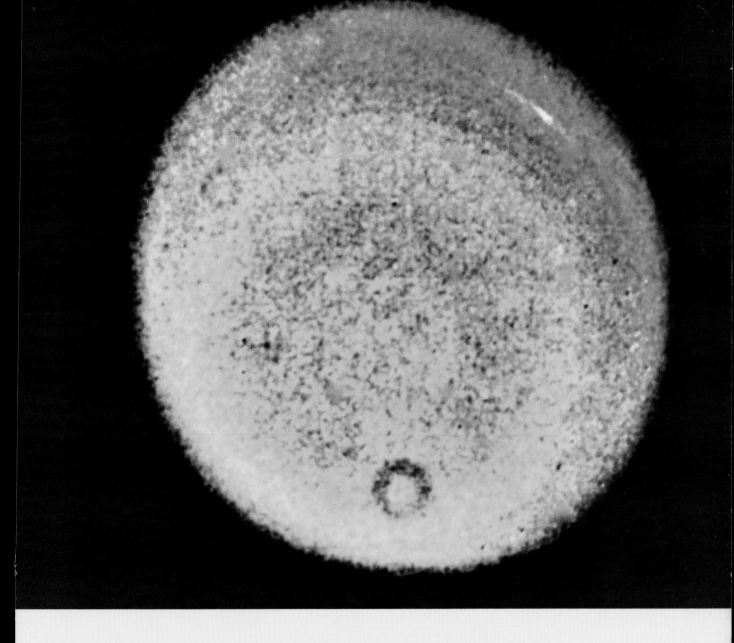

Uranus is so far from the Earth that you need a
telescope to see it. Uranus has rings like Saturn, but
they are thinner. Uranus rotates in a strange way—
sideways! If the Earth rotated like Uranus, the north
and south poles would each be pointing toward the
Sun for half the year.

Uranus's moons seem to have surfaces of dirty ice, with many craters and valleys like our moon. Below is the dark, icy surface of the moon named Miranda.

On Neptune, you would need thicker fur than a polar bear to keep warm. It's a frozen ball of ice!

BRRRRR !!!

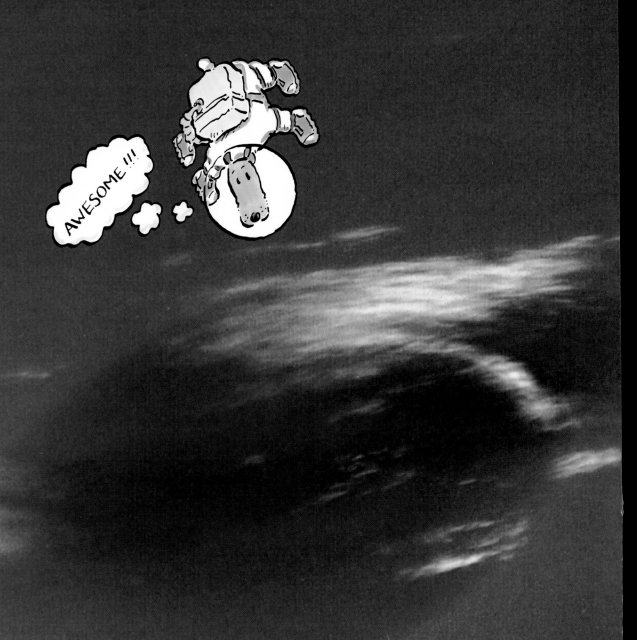

Until the spacecraft *Voyager 2* sent back pictures of Neptune, very little was known about the planet. The most exciting discovery about Neptune was the Great Dark Spot. This spot is a huge storm, just like the Great Red Spot on Jupiter.

The farthest planet from the Sun, Pluto, was not discovered until 1930. It has one moon, Charon, and is coated with ice. Not only is Pluto the coldest planet, but it also has a strange orbit. Every so often, Pluto swings inside the orbit of Neptune and gets closer to the Sun than Neptune. But don't worry. There's no chance that the two planets will ever bump into each other!

Isn't there an easier way to find a planet?

Of course. Just go outside right now.

What's this?

Why, you're standing on it right now.

This is your very own planet!
It's the planet EARTH!

GLOSSARY

astronomer: A scientist who is interested in explaining how the universe works, and who observes and studies the planets, stars, and galaxies for this purpose.

carbon dioxide: A colorless gas made up of a combination of carbon and oxygen. The oxygen in the air we breathe *in* changes to the carbon dioxide we breathe *out.*

constellation: One of a number of patterns of fixed stars in the sky that are often named after animals, gods, or mythical heroes

craters: Circle-shaped hollows caused by the impact of meteors and other objects hitting the surface of planets or moons

planetarium: Usually a building where images of the planets, constellations, or other parts of the universe are projected onto a screen

Solar System: The Sun and all the bodies that move around it—planets, moons, comets, asteriods, and meteors

telescope: An instrument used by astronomers to observe planets, stars, and galaxies